Help the mail carrier deliver the letters.

Start

Finish

733

Get to the finish without getting sprayed by the skunk!

Start

Finish

2

Help the scientist with his experiment.

Start

Finish

Get to the finish without getting wet!

Start

Finish

Help the hamster get through the maze to his bed.

Help the mouse get to the plate of cheese.

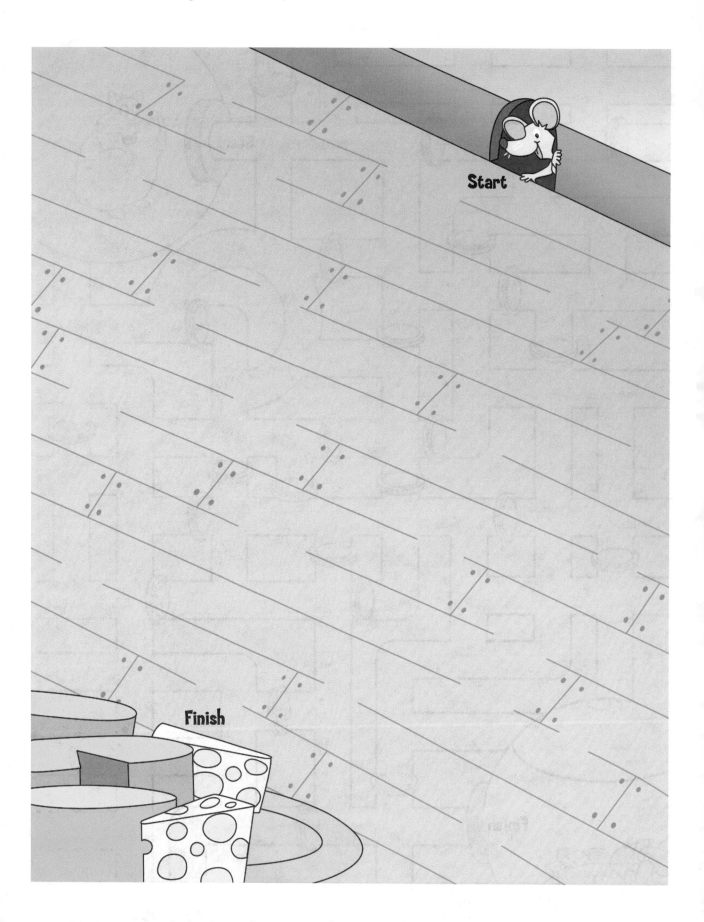

Help the taxi get to the hotel.

Help the dog get back to his house.

Start

Finish

Help the rabbit get to the carrots.

Start

Finish

Help the squid swim through the water.

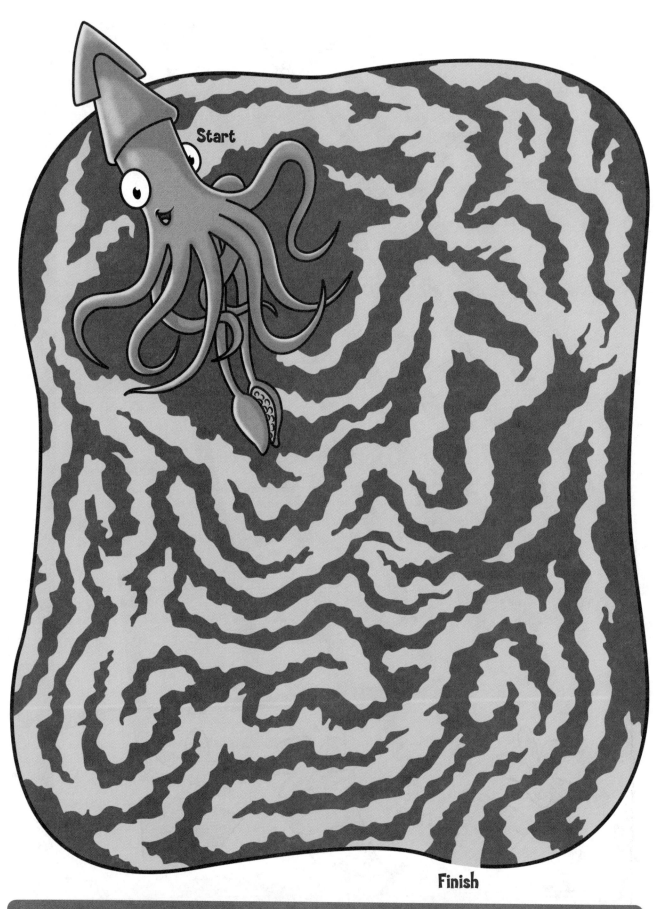

Start

Finish

Help get the ball into the goal.

11

Help get the ball to the pins.

Finish

Start

Help the horse get across the pasture.

Start

Finish

Help the boy shut off his alarm clock.

Start

Finish

Help the rocket get to the orange planet.

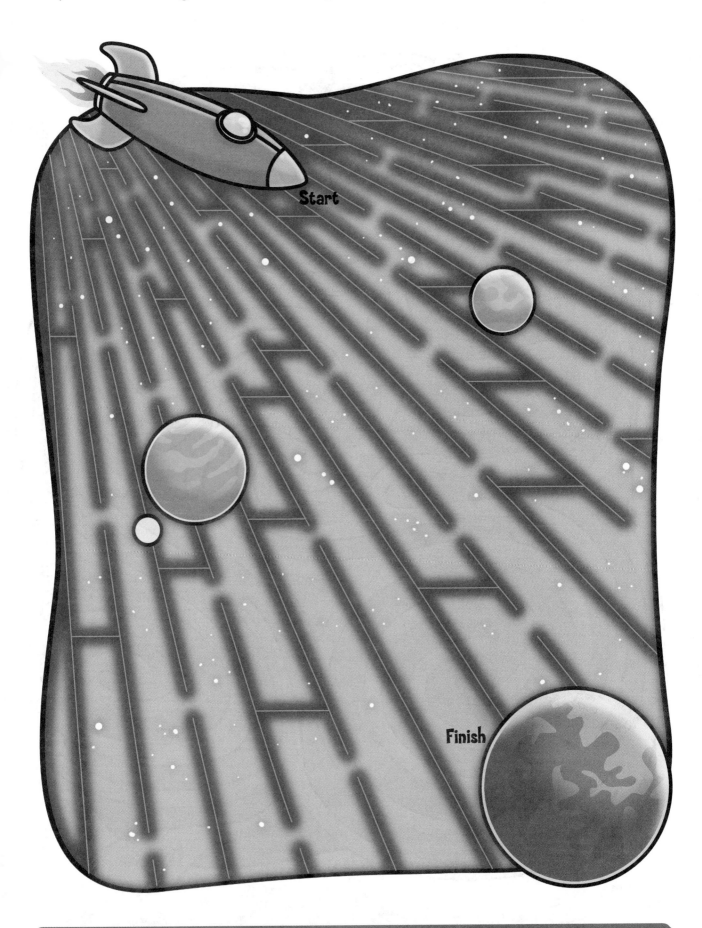

Start

Finish

Help the toucan move through the rain forest.

Start

Finish

Help the police officer get to the traffic jam.

Help plug in the gorilla's hair dryer.

Help the squirrel gather the acorns.

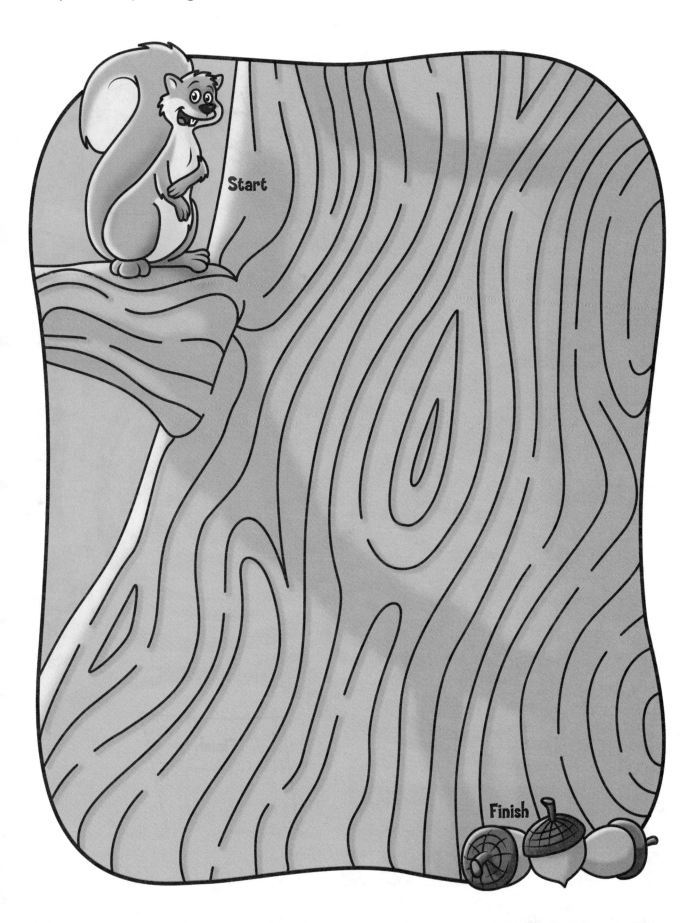

Help the racer reach the finish line.

Start

Finish

Help the fisherman catch the fish.

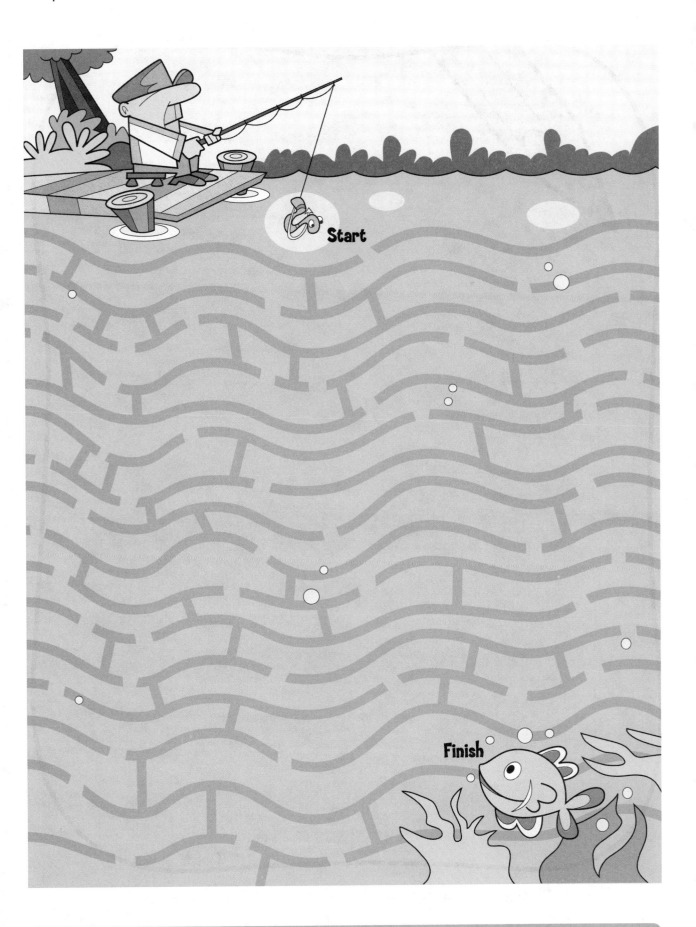

Start

Finish

Help the pencil get to the bottom of the page.

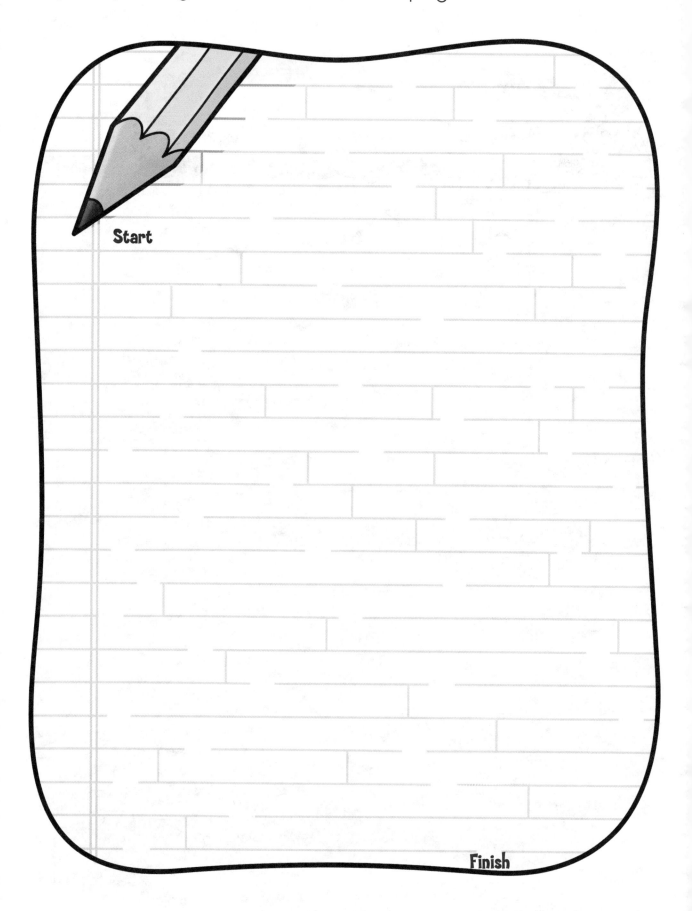

Start

Finish

Help the robot get to the tools he needs.

Start

Finish

Help the girl paddle down the river. Watch out for rocks!

Start

Finish

Help the caterpillar get to the butterfly.

Start

Finish

Help the ant get to the watermelon.

Help the turtle get to the ocean floor.

Start

Finish

Help the waiter bring the drink to the lady.

Help the seagull get to the piece of popcorn.

Start

Finish

Help the worm get to his underground home.

Start

Finish

Help the ladybug get to the flower.

Start

Finish

Help the monkey get to the banana.

Help the ship get to its home.

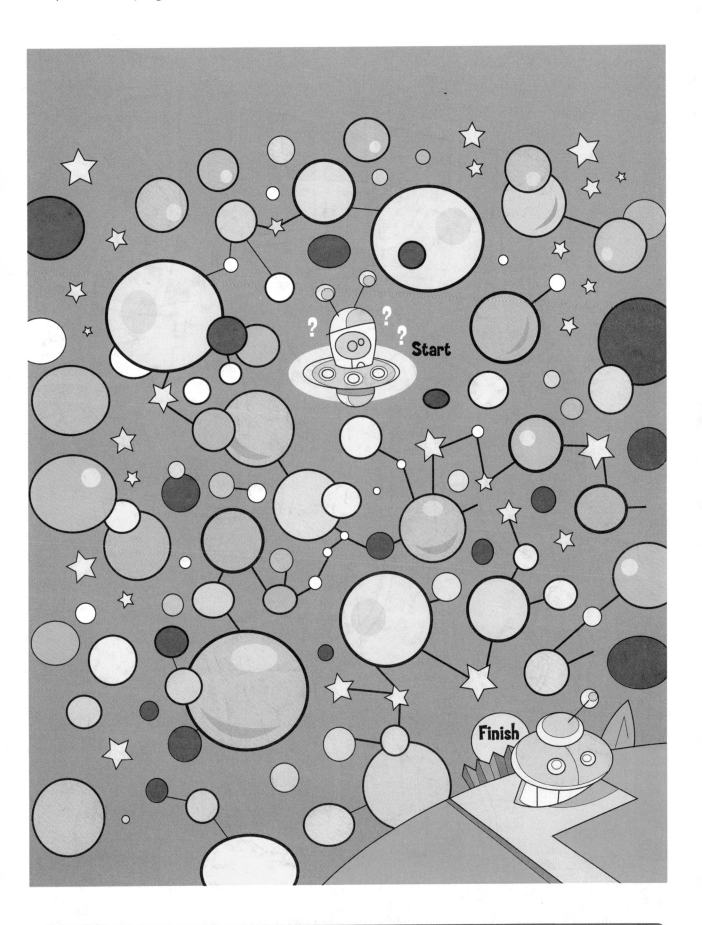

Help the climber get to the top of the cliff.

Help get the cue ball to the eight ball.

Help the pilot land the plane.

Help the train reach the traveler.

Start

Finish

Help get the hot air balloon to the landing pad.

Start

Finish

Help get the hermit crab to the sand castle.

Start

Finish

Help the cow get to the barn.

Finish

Start

Help the polar bear get to the other side of the iceberg.

Help the lion get to the lion cub!

Help the elephant get to the umbrella.

Help the golfer putt the golf ball into the hole.

Start

Finish

Help the knight get to the dragon.

Start

Finish

Help the goldfish find the treasure.

Start

Finish

Help the plane get to the gate.

Help the giraffe get through the forest.

Start

Finish

Help the kicker get the football through the uprights.

Help the superhero rescue the cat!

Start

Finish

Help the spider find his glasses.

Start

Finish

Help the hiker get to the ledge.

Help the snowman find his carrot nose.

Start

Finish

Help the dog get to the fire hydrant.

Finish

Start

Help the chipmunk find the acorn.

Start

Finish

Help the skateboarder get to the bottom of the ramp.

Find the way through the super maze cube!

Note: Only one solution is shown for each maze, but other paths are possible.

Page 1

Page 2

Page 3

Page 4

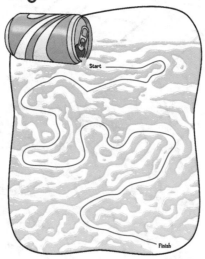

Page 5

Page 6

Page 7

Page 8

Note: Only one solution is shown for each maze, but other paths are possible.

Page 9

Page 10

Page 11

Page 12

Page 13

Page 14

Page 15

Page 16

Note: Only one solution is shown for each maze, but other paths are possible.

Page 17

Page 18

Page 19

Page 20

Page 21

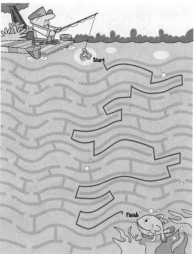

Page 22

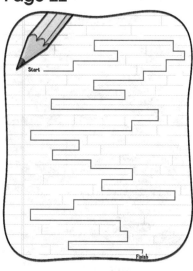

Page 23

Page 24

Note: Only one solution is shown for each maze, but other paths are possible.

Page 25

Page 26

Page 27

Page 28

Page 29

Page 30

Page 31

Page 32

Note: Only one solution is shown for each maze, but other paths are possible.

Page 33

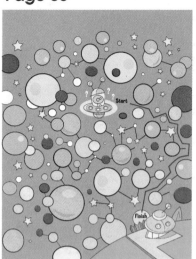

Page 34

Page 35

Page 36

Page 37

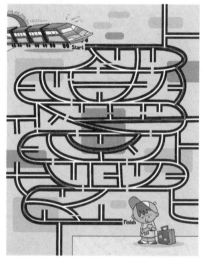

Page 38

Page 39

Page 40

Note: Only one solution is shown for each maze, but other paths are possible.

Page 41

Page 42

Page 43

Page 44

Page 45

Page 46

Page 47

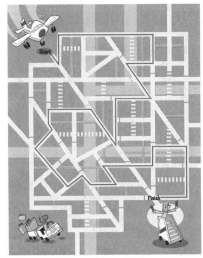

Page 48

Note: Only one solution is shown for each maze, but other paths are possible

Page 49

Page 50

Page 51

Page 52

Page 53

Page 54

Page 55

Page 56

Page 57

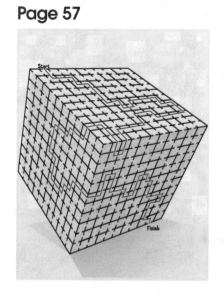

Mazes 08231